SHIPS AND SUBMARINES

Design	Cooper-West
Editor	Denny Robson
Researcher	Cecilia Weston-Baker
Illustrators	Rob Shone and Cooper-West
Consultant	Michael Corkhill, Member of the Royal Institution of Naval Architects, UK

Copyright © 1987 by Aladdin Books Limited
An Aladdin Book
Designed and directed by Aladdin Books Limited
70 Old Compton Street, London W1

Published by Price/Stern/Sloan Publishers, Inc.
360 North La Cienega Boulevard, Los Angeles, California 90048

ISBN: 0-8431-4289-8

THE **HOW AND WHY** WONDER BOOK® OF

SHIPS AND SUBMARINES

MICHAEL GREY

PRICE/STERN/SLOAN

Publishers, Inc., Los Angeles

1987

The hull of a ship under construction

Foreword

Compared to the elegant ships of the past, modern vessels look rather ugly and functional. They are, however, products of great changes in maritime technology which have taken place during the past 20 years. This has been a period which has seen the development of containerships, roll-on roll-off ferries (ro-ros), giant gas carriers and tankers, together with a whole range of strange craft designed for the new offshore industries. This book looks at the technology behind these ships. It also examines the developments that have taken place in naval vessels, which have been dominated by advances in weapons systems and the evolution of today's huge, silent submarines.

Contents

Today's ships and submarines

The merchant ship has always been the most effective carrier of goods in the world, but modern craft have reached new levels of efficiency. The latest types of merchant ships can carry many times the cargo of previous years, using much less fuel and with a crew only a fraction of the size previously required. All this has been accomplished by new designs of ship, advanced techniques in cargo handling to cut down time in port and the latest developments in automation and shipboard electronics. Modern warships have been developed to fulfil many military roles in many different areas. Moreover, today's navies have switched their attention from above the waves to below, with greater emphasis on sophisticated attack and missile submarines.

1 Propulsion

Modern merchant ships are driven by slow or medium-speed diesel engines, as these are the most economical. A slow-speed engine drives the propeller directly, while a medium-speed engine drives through a gearbox. Cheap, heavy fuel oil is used. Waste heat is converted into electrical power by passing exhaust gases through a "turbo-generator."

2 Navigation

In modern ships navigation is controlled by electronic systems. The vessel is controlled from the bridge. Anti-collision radar, satellite navigation equipment and echo sounders are all important sensors.

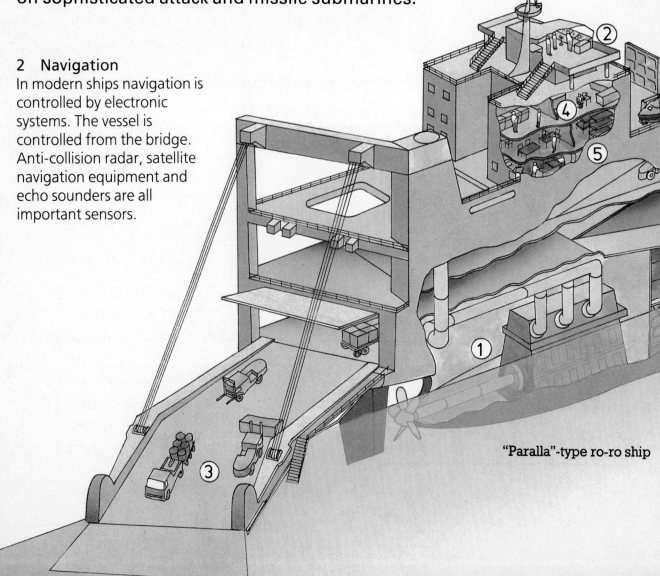

"Paralla"-type ro-ro ship

3 Cargo handling

The ship's time in port is governed by her cargo handling equipment, which therefore has to be extremely efficient. Some ships depend upon shore equipment for their cargo handling, while others are fitted with their own cranes or "derricks." The vessel shown below uses a system of ramps, tractors and fork-lift trucks to load and discharge.

4 Computers

In modern ships computers are used in navigation, data monitoring, cargo calculations and in the monitoring of maintenance and spares systems. Computer readouts give the course, speed and estimated time to the next change of course. They can even be programmed to steer the ship across the ocean and to govern engine speeds for an exact time of arrival.

5 Accommodation

Because the crews on most modern ships are small in number, it is usually possible to give everyone on board his own cabin.

6 Materials

The hull of a modern ship is made of steel, reinforced in the more vulnerable areas where the full force of the sea is felt, such as the bow and stern.

Ships, submarines and their systems

Every ship and submarine is a collection of materials and systems, designed to carry a certain amount of cargo at a specified speed and dimensions. Other important factors are the daily running costs and the size of the crew which is needed. The diagram on this page illustrates one of the latest types of deepsea roll-on, roll-off containerships. She can handle her cargo without relying on port equipment by using the huge access ramp at the stern. Such ships trade worldwide with a variety of cargo.

Design and building

Ships and submarines are designed by naval architects, who must take into account many different requirements. The ship's hullform, particularly under water, must be smooth to minimize resistance and stable in all conditions. If it is a merchant ship, it must be full-bodied enough to economically carry a useful payload at a reasonable speed. If it is a warship, it must be habitable in extreme conditions, fast and an adequate weapon platform.

Test tanks and computer-aided design

As part of the design process, scale models are used to test the seakeeping ability of a ship in a "test tank." Computers are also used in this process, as they enable various designs to be tested without having to be built first. Computers are also used in drafting building plans for the shipyard and in cutting steel.

Building the ship

Modern shipyards build sections of the ship inside assembly halls. These sections are then put together and fitted out under cover.

▽ The photograph shows a model of a heavy lift ship in a test tank. Tank testing is an essential part of the ship design process. Scale models made of wax or wood are tested with very strong wave forces to measure their seakeeping qualities.

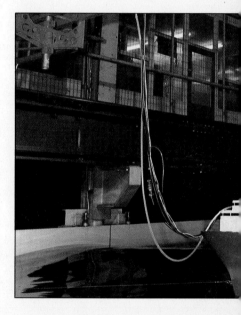

◁ The use of computers saves many hundreds of manhours in design offices and shipyards. Computer programs are available which will direct steel cutting and preparation machinery. A "three-dimensional" effect, illustrated in the photograph, can be obtained to help in designing the ship.

▷ Advances in propeller design have greatly improved propulsion efficiency. The Grims Vane Wheel shown here is mounted on the shaft behind the propeller. It improves the flow of water and reduces turbulence.

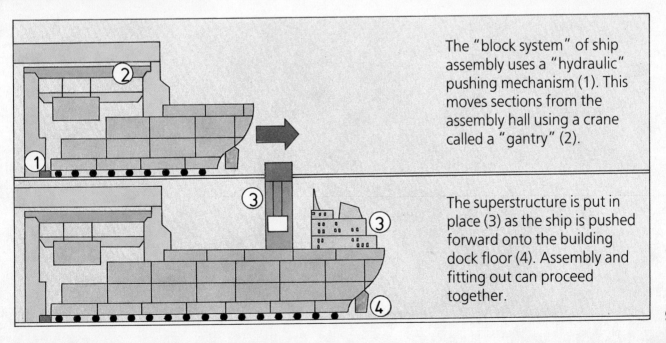

The "block system" of ship assembly uses a "hydraulic" pushing mechanism (1). This moves sections from the assembly hall using a crane called a "gantry" (2).

The superstructure is put in place (3) as the ship is pushed forward onto the building dock floor (4). Assembly and fitting out can proceed together.

Ship propulsion

The choice of propulsion decides how fast a ship can travel and how economic it is to run. Nuclear power is used in large warships and submarines, as it enables them to operate for long periods without refueling. Gas turbine machinery is also used in warships, where high sprint speeds are demanded. In the last few years, fuel efficiency has become more important and many advances have taken place, such as the development of wind-assisted ships.

The economical diesel

However, for merchant ships the main advances concern diesel engine design. The latest designs are able to operate with low-quality oil very economically. Giant energy-efficient bulk carriers, fitted with a modern large diesel engine, are able to haul 200,000 tons of cargo using only 50-60 tons of fuel per day. This is less than one-third the amount needed 10 years ago.

▽ Some of the options for ship propulsion include the economical diesel, the gas turbine, along with its turbo-electric version for fast warships and nuclear power which provides great endurance.

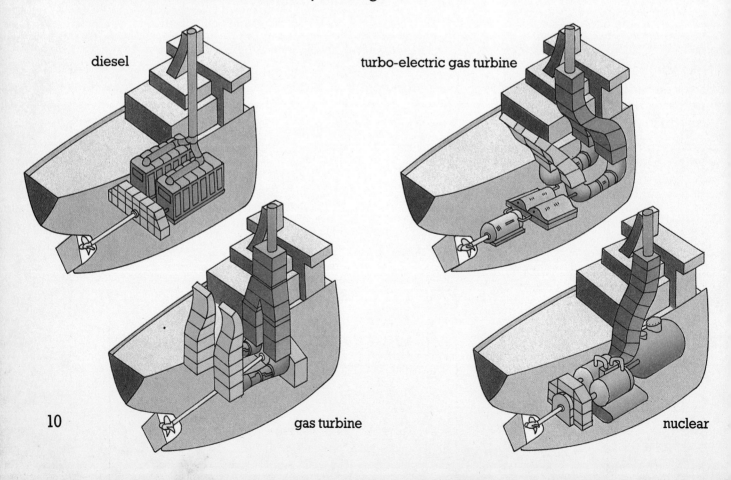

diesel

turbo-electric gas turbine

gas turbine

nuclear

This Japanese design of a wind-assisted ship has been used for ships of up to 30,000 tons. It uses a computer to "blend" sails and engine to achieve the greatest economy at the desired speed. The wind direction and speed (1) are assessed by a sensor on top of the mast (2), which gives this information to the computer (3) on the bridge. The computer then sends a signal to the sail mechanism to "trim" the sails most efficiently (4) and to vary the engine (5) revolutions to operate most economically. The sails are folded in half when not in use. They can be used in hurricane force winds and save up to 30 per cent in fuel costs.

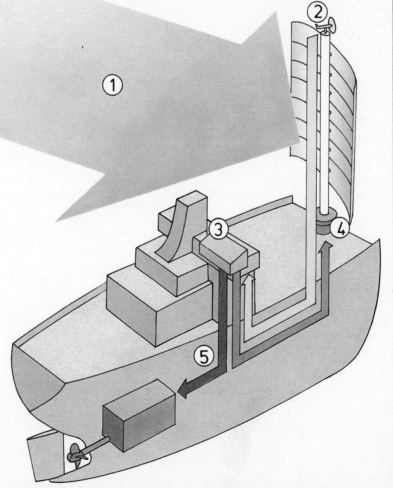

Navigation and communications

Important new developments in navigation equipment have made it possible to operate ships with smaller crews. A large merchant ship today will normally be controlled by a single watchkeeping officer on the bridge. In addition to his navigational duties, the officer is able to monitor the engine room by remote control. Long-range radio navigation aids and satellite navigation equipment give him an "instant" position by night or day. Computer-assisted radar helps with collision avoidance by automatically plotting the positions of other ships. Consequently a schedule can be kept to even in poor visibility, such as at night or in bad weather conditions.

◁ The computer has become an important part of the modern ship's equipment. The Databridge equipment seen here provides the officer of the watch with a wealth of information. Data is provided on collision avoidance and a variety of readouts on the ship's position, the course to steer and a complete monitoring facility for the state of the main engines. It can be linked to other computers which assist in the ship's everyday business and in record-keeping.

The ship's sensors

Satellites have revolutionized navigation and communications. In this diagram both ships are able to precisely establish their position using "Satnav" (satellite navigation) (1).

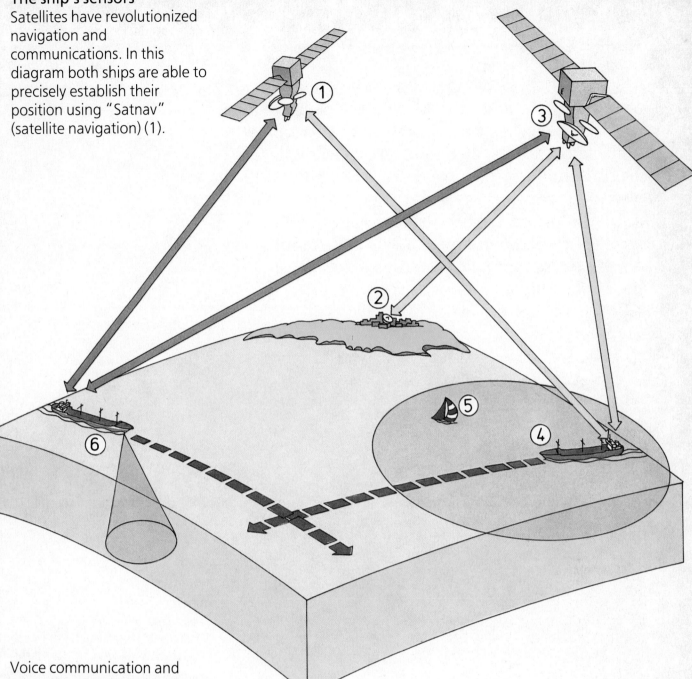

Voice communication and telex messages between the ships and their head office (2) are improved by a communications satellite (3). Anti-collision radar aboard the right-hand ship (4) has detected the presence of a yacht (5) and calculated a course necessary to clear it. "Guard rings" on the radar make a noise, giving warning that another ship is nearby. The other ship (6) is monitoring the depth of the sea using "sonar."

Keeping in touch

The use of satellite communication equipment has greatly improved how precisely ships can operate. The ship management company can now communicate with its ships anywhere in the world, through normal telex and telephone links. The performance of the ship's machinery can be monitored from the owner's office. Distress and emergency procedures are more effective because of reliable communications.

Ports

The modern port ideally provides all-weather access for shipping, with deep water at all stages of the tide. High-speed cargo handling facilities are also important, as a ship is not earning when she is not under way. A "vessel traffic control system" directs shipping in the port approaches and port waters. It provides computerized information to everyone dealing with shipping in the port and is a modern feature that greatly improves port efficiency.

◁ In the port's vessel traffic control system, radar monitors vessel movements while a communications system provides information to agents, pilots and port emergency services.

Special terminals

Today, the tendency is toward specialized terminals within the port, which handle one particular type of ship or trade. It is not unusual for a large containership, using a special terminal equipped with modern gantry cranes, to be turned around in a single tide! A modern bulk terminal could discharge a 100,000-ton cargo of coal in two working days, using "grabs" able to lift 70 tons in a single bite.

▷ Profile of a port. Tugs maneuver a large ro-ro ship (1) alongside the container/ro-ro berths (2). Two deepsea containerships (3) work cargo at their own specialized terminal. General cargo is collected in the covered sheds (4) for distribution by road. The container berths are next to a train terminal (5).

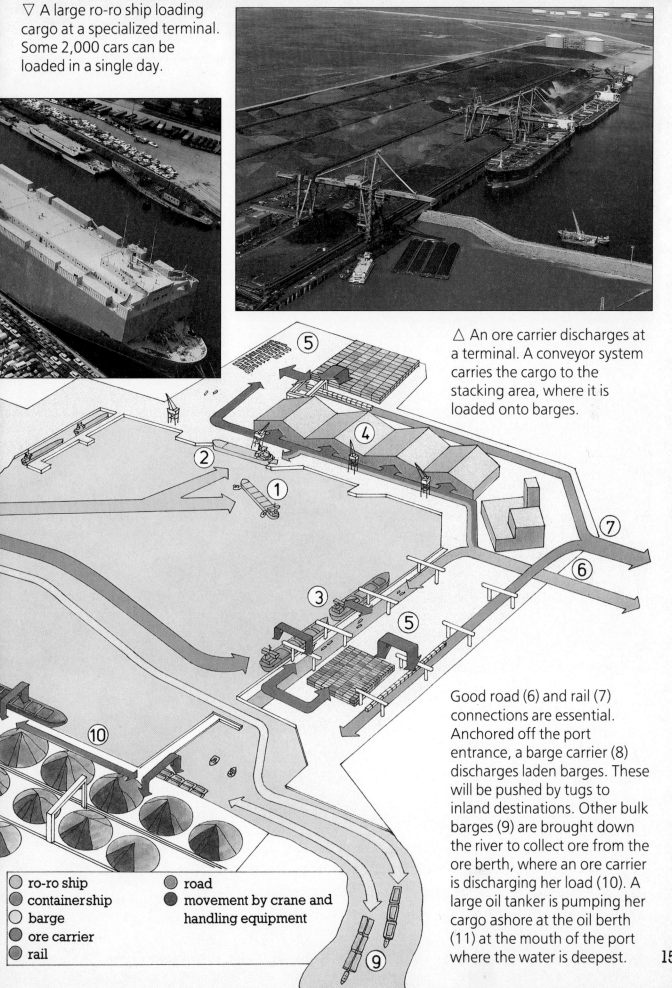

▽ A large ro-ro ship loading cargo at a specialized terminal. Some 2,000 cars can be loaded in a single day.

△ An ore carrier discharges at a terminal. A conveyor system carries the cargo to the stacking area, where it is loaded onto barges.

Good road (6) and rail (7) connections are essential. Anchored off the port entrance, a barge carrier (8) discharges laden barges. These will be pushed by tugs to inland destinations. Other bulk barges (9) are brought down the river to collect ore from the ore berth, where an ore carrier is discharging her load (10). A large oil tanker is pumping her cargo ashore at the oil berth (11) at the mouth of the port where the water is deepest.

- ● ro-ro ship
- ● container ship
- ● barge
- ● ore carrier
- ● rail
- ● road
- ● movement by crane and handling equipment

Containerships and barge carriers

The use of 20-foot and 40-foot containers throughout the world has greatly improved transport efficiency. These units go from factory to factory without being opened. Specialized containerships, with "cells" to hold the boxes securely, have virtually taken over the world's deepsea cargo liner routes. Smaller "feeder" ships distribute containers to and from the main ports where large terminals have been built. The largest containerships are able to hold up to 4,000 20-foot boxes, although 2,000-3,000 unit vessels are more common.

▽ One of the latest Taiwanese Evergreen containerships coming into port. Because the containers themselves are weatherproof, it is possible to stow large numbers on top of the hatches as deck cargo. This ship is able to hold more than 3,000 containers, and depends on shore cranes to load and discharge when she reaches port.

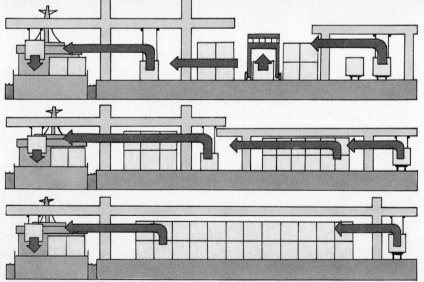

◁ Different layouts of container terminal. At the top, a small gantry lifts boxes off railroad cars for transfer into the stack by straddle carrier. This then delivers the box under the main gantry which loads it onto the ship. In the middle layout, the right-hand gantry spans the container stack and delivers the box to the ship's crane. In the layout below, all handling is by a single gantry.

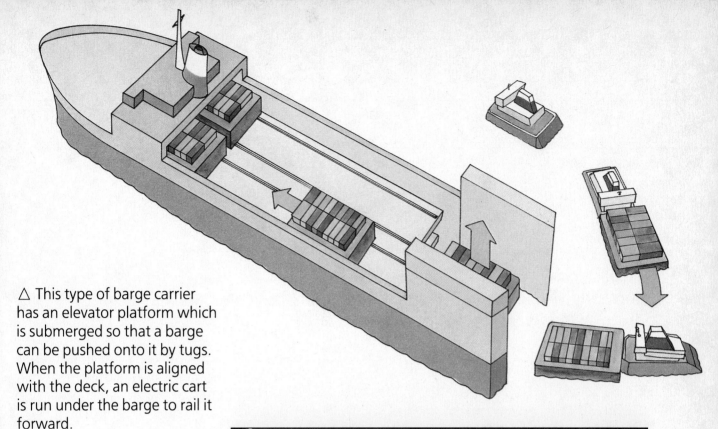

△ This type of barge carrier has an elevator platform which is submerged so that a barge can be pushed onto it by tugs. When the platform is aligned with the deck, an electric cart is run under the barge to rail it forward.

▷ Other types of barge carrier are "ballasted" down to allow barge trains to be pushed into them through huge bow doors. The vessel in the photograph is of the LASH (Lighter Aboard Ship) type. It uses a giant gantry crane to pick barges up out of the water under the stern. The laden crane then rolls forward to place the barges in the vessel's holds or in on-deck storage positions.

Container handling

While some ships working in the developing world are equipped with their own gantry cranes, most containerships depend upon large port cranes and ground-handling equipment. Cranes called "straddle carriers" and large fork-lift trucks are used to transfer containers on the wharf. Still bigger transport units are handled by barge carriers. This type of ship can carry very heavy loads – up to 800 tons – quite independently of port facilities. This gives them special advantages in less-developed countries.

Tankers

There are a number of quite distinctive types of tanker. The largest are the very large crude carriers (VLCCs) that work the long-haul crude oil routes. Such vessels today are seldom over 250,000 tons. Product tankers range up to 80,000 tons and carry refined oil cargoes. Chemical and parcel tankers are highly sophisticated ships able to carry up to 50 different types of cargo simultaneously, from acids to edible oils.

Gas tankers

Gas carriers are a particularly specialized type of tanker which carry cargoes of liquefied natural gas (LNG) or liquefied petroleum gas (LPG). The gas is carried either under pressure in steel tanks, or refrigerated at temperatures as low as −165°C (−265°F) in tanks made of special steels or aluminum.

▽ The photograph on the left is of a LNG tanker while the photograph on the right shows the inside of a LNG tank. LNG is carried at extremely low temperatures in either spherical or prismatic-shaped tanks, which are surrounded by thick layers of insulation. Special grades of steel or aluminum must be used for the tanks themselves to cope with the intense cold and to enable the tank walls to expand and contract.

Handling giant ships

The collision or grounding of a ship carrying a full load of oil, gases or chemicals could have terrible results. Consequently, every precaution is taken to minimize such risks. "Simulator training," where the exact handling characteristics of a large ship can be reproduced, is used to train crew and pilots.

▽ A bridge simulator uses computer-generated imagery to reproduce conditions in a specific port approach location. Working controls, noise and vibration help to simulate a real situation.

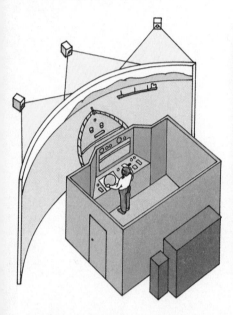

Passenger ships and ferries

Cruise vessels, catering for the holiday trade, have taken over from the old passenger liners as the most glamorous ships in the world. The emphasis is on super luxury, with every passenger having the facilities of a top-class hotel, complete with high-quality entertainment. So it is not surprising that these ships are the world's most expensive merchant ships.

▽ The top photograph shows the British *Royal Princess*. This ship set new standards of luxury when she was delivered for the US cruise market. Because of the multi-deck arrangement, all passengers can enjoy a sea view with outside berths. There are also whole suites of rooms higher up on the vessel.

The photograph below shows one of the giant ferries which serves the Baltic Sea trades. A modern ferry provides first-class facilities for passengers and their cars, besides carrying a large number of trucks and trailers. It is able to load and discharge a complete "cargo" through its bow and stern doors in well under an hour.

Such vessels cost even more than the largest LNG carrier. For example, the P & O Shipping Line paid $210 million for its *Royal Princess.*

Enter the superferries

Ferries, most of which carry cars and trucks in addition to passengers are, in their most modern form, highly sophisticated ships. These vessels offer cruise liner comfort for up to 1,500 passengers. A fast turnaround in port is usually required by ferry operators and, for extra speed, cargo is often able to drive through the vessel using bow and stern doors. Because of the unique designs of hovercraft – which travel on a "cushion" of air – and hydrofoil, they are now used very successfully for high-speed ferry links.

▽ The Boeing Jetfoil is used for high-speed ferry operations in many areas of the world. A service speed of 40 knots can be maintained. A smooth ride in rough seas is ensured by the use of the sonic height sensor (1), which, through its computer (2), automatically controls the surfaces on the steerable bow foil (3). The foils may be retracted when the craft is hullborne. The craft is driven by gas turbines (4), which draw water into the system through a pod beneath the hull (5). The water is expelled at great velocity through water jet nozzles (6).

Boeing Jetfoil

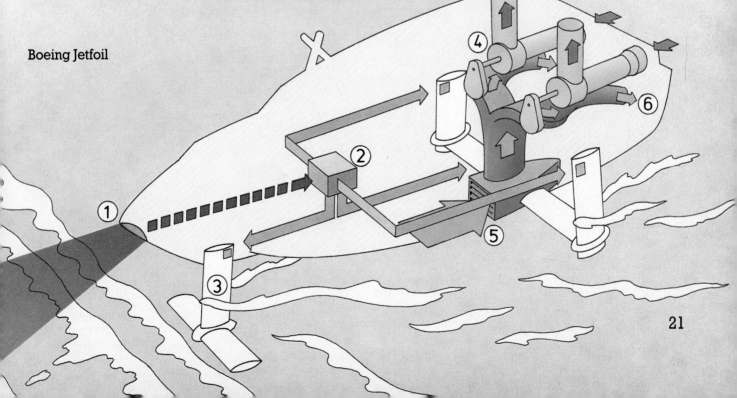

Warships

Naval strategists and their designers have to be concerned with national defense, the protection of merchant shipping and control of sea routes. A more recent consideration is the special use of submarines in modern warfare. All warships, from the aircraft carrier group to the more humble minesweeper, are designed and operated with these considerations in mind.

▽ The modern warship provides a "platform" for a number of modular systems. Different types of ship can be made up depending on the combination of systems used. They include the engine, electronics, gun units, anti-submarine, surface-to-surface and surface-to-air systems.

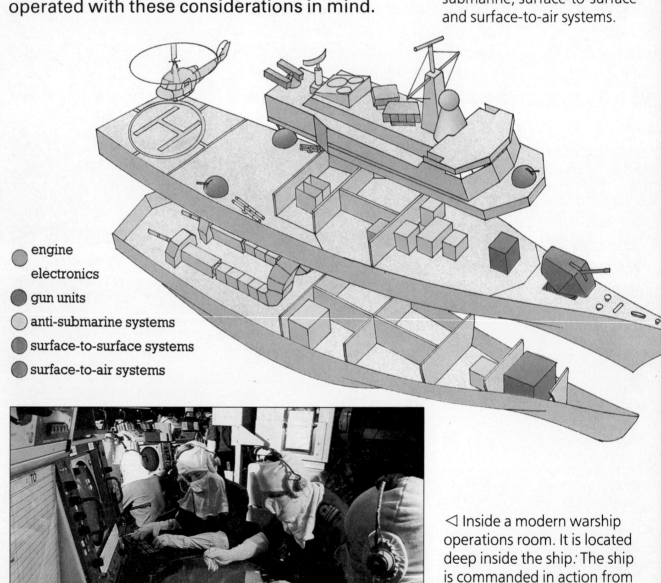

- ● engine
- electronics
- ● gun units
- ◯ anti-submarine systems
- ● surface-to-surface systems
- ◉ surface-to-air systems

◁ Inside a modern warship operations room. It is located deep inside the ship. The ship is commanded in action from here and all the vessel's electronic sensors are to be found in this room. The personnel are shown wearing protective clothing to guard them against burns in the event of an explosion.

Electronic warfare, the use of guided weapons and the nuclear-powered submarine are the three keys to modern naval strategy. Electronics provide the sensors to detect an enemy and the computers to out-think him. The electronic brains of a warship are now more expensive than the vessel itself! The use of guided weapons has carried the effective range of a warship far over the horizon. Nuclear power and weapons have provided the submarine with its frightening ability to act as both a deterrent and "ship killer."

▽ This ship is one of the latest types of mine-hunter. It can run silently to search out mines. Such vessels are often made of non-magnetic material, such as glass fiber, to combat magnetic mines. They are also able to operate robot submersibles to search out and destroy mines on the sea bottom.

▷ Profile of the modern fleet showing the aircraft carrier (1), screened by missile cruisers (2) and anti-submarine forces of frigates (3) and destroyers (4). These also provide defense against surface and air attack. An assault vessel (5) launches both helicopters and its landing craft (6). Support ships keep the warships refueled (7), while submarines (8) patrol beyond the horizon.

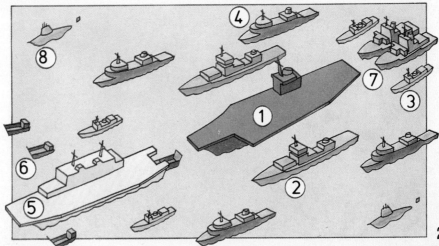

Submarines

Modern submarines are either diesel electric or nuclear-powered. Nuclear-powered subs are divided into hunter/killer submarines, which are attack craft, and ballistic missile-carrying subs, or SSBNs. Hunter/killers are designed to attack other submarines or surface vessels. They are armed with torpedoes and short-range missiles. The SSBN serves as a platform for guided missiles carrying nuclear warheads. These submarines hide somewhere in the world's oceans and act as a deterrent to any country threatening a "first strike" with nuclear weapons.

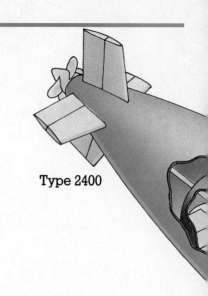

Type 2400

Submarine weapons

SSBNs are armed with submarine-launched ballistic missiles, such as Polaris or Trident. Low-flying Cruise missiles are also carried aboard some submarines. Hunter/killer submarines are armed with torpedoes, anti-submarine missiles and anti-surface ship missiles. The largest submarines now entering service are the Soviet Navy's "Typhoon" class of SSBN.

△ This is the Soviet Navy's new 30,000 ton missile-carrying "Typhoon" submarine. It carries intercontinental ballistic missiles. This huge nuclear-powered craft is more than 200 meters (600 feet) in length. It is seen as the Soviet Union's answer to the US Navy's Trident-armed "Ohio" class of SSBN.

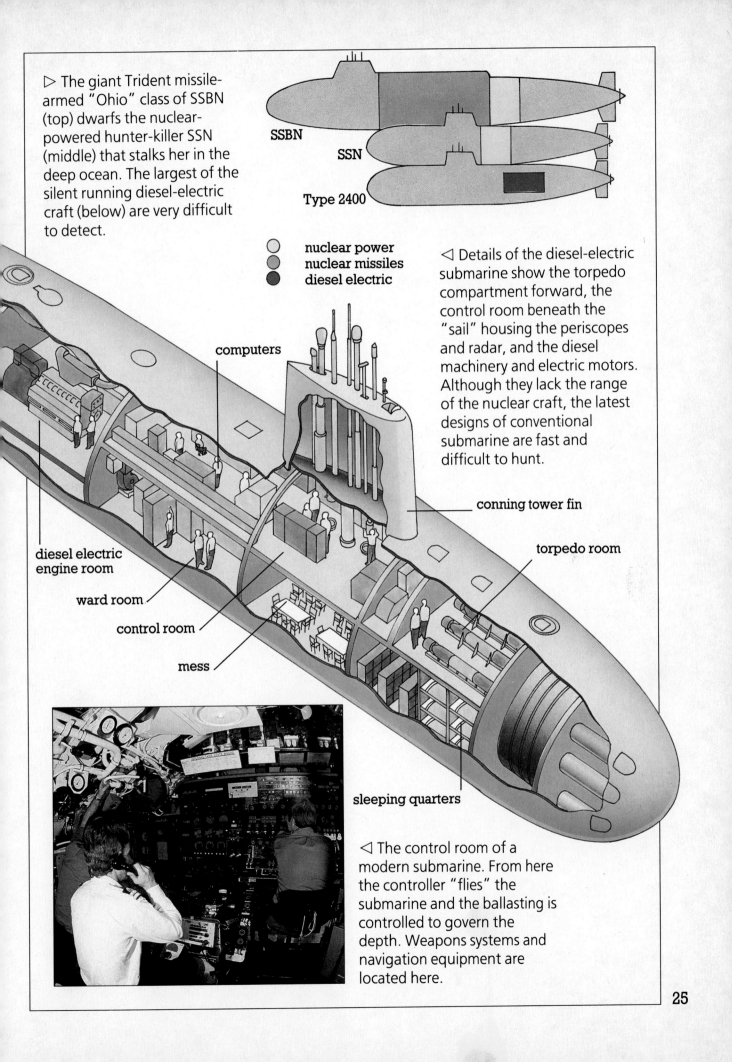

▷ The giant Trident missile-armed "Ohio" class of SSBN (top) dwarfs the nuclear-powered hunter-killer SSN (middle) that stalks her in the deep ocean. The largest of the silent running diesel-electric craft (below) are very difficult to detect.

SSBN

SSN

Type 2400

- nuclear power
- nuclear missiles
- diesel electric

◁ Details of the diesel-electric submarine show the torpedo compartment forward, the control room beneath the "sail" housing the periscopes and radar, and the diesel machinery and electric motors. Although they lack the range of the nuclear craft, the latest designs of conventional submarine are fast and difficult to hunt.

computers

conning tower fin

torpedo room

diesel electric engine room

ward room

control room

mess

sleeping quarters

◁ The control room of a modern submarine. From here the controller "flies" the submarine and the ballasting is controlled to govern the depth. Weapons systems and navigation equipment are located here.

Special ships

The salvage of damaged vessels, the transport of very heavy or large loads, the specialist demands of the offshore oil industry and the maintenance of shipping routes in heavy ice all demand special ships exclusively designed for the job. Consequently, all these craft have very individual characteristics. A large salvage tug has enormous power and heavy pumping capacity. An ice breaker is hugely reinforced and exceptionally maneuverable. Craft designed for the offshore industry have unusual stability.

Heavy lifters

Some of the most spectacular vessels at sea today are to be found in the heavy lift fleet. These ships earn their living transporting exceptionally heavy loads, such as drilling rigs or sections for offshore platforms. Some of these craft depend on cranes capable of lifting individual loads of up to 1,500 tons. However, others can actually submerge beneath a floating load and then surface to pick up the cargo! A 10,000-ton load would not be unusual for such ships.

▽ Finland's latest icebreaker, the brand new *Otso*, features a stainless steel hull that does not require painting. It also has an air-bubbling system that lubricates the hull in ice to reduce friction and enormous power capable of driving the craft through thick ice.

Heavy lift ships

Exceptionally heavy or large single loads are carried around the world by a specialist fleet of heavy lift ships. Some use very heavy derricks to lift loads of up to 600 tons. Others are designed like ro-ro vessels and can handle multi-wheeled or tracked vehicles. Power station and refinery plant, offshore rig sections and heavy railroad stock are frequently carried by this type of ship.

▽ A new type of self-propelled heavy lifter (1) has been developed to carry very large floating objects safely on deepsea voyages. The craft ballasts down to submerge the main cargo deck (2) allowing the load to be floated over. Water is then pumped out allowing the load (in this case it is an oil rig) to "ground" on the deck, where it is secured for the voyage.

The future

More efficient hullforms, the use of robots, remote-controlled ships and giant cargo-carrying submarines are all being explored by naval architects for future generations of ships. Plastics may replace steel as the main construction material within 50 years. New means of propulsion may include "electromagnetic generation" and more use of wind power. As well as sails, wind turbines and even kites are being studied to supplement diesel power.

▽ Both these designs are for super-luxury "resort ships." Such ships of the future could be fitted with harbors for watersports and stationed in beautiful locations, moving only with the seasons.

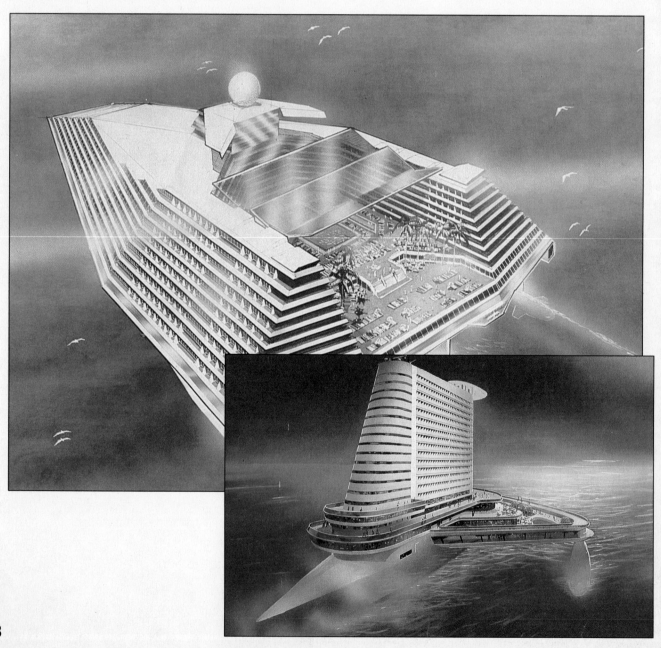

▽ For future generations of ship, designers are already looking at the use of high-altitude kites or sails to supplement the ship's engines, semisubmersible hulls to provide huge deck areas and even completely wind-powered craft, driven by giant turbines.

Amazing designs of cruise ship have already been developed. Designers have also been studying the idea of semisubmersible catamarans, which are thought to offer a good compromise for ships requiring both speed and stability. To save manpower on long ocean voyages, a robot-controlled convoy with a single manned "mothership" watching over its progress is another attractive idea to ship designers. For military purposes, however, performance will continue to be the guiding principle, while future developments in cargo ships will be concerned with economy rather than speed.

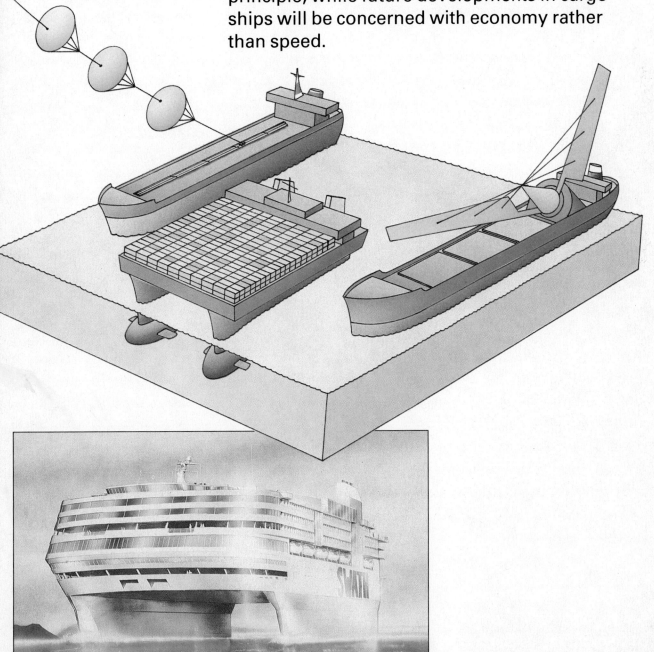

Datechart

1802

Charlotte Dundas, the world's first reliable steamship, goes into operation on the Forth & Clyde Canal, Scotland.

1900

John P. Holland forms the Electric Boat Company to build the first successful submarines in the US.

1912

The world's first seagoing motorship powered by diesel engines is built.

1912

The transatlantic liner *Titanic* sinks after striking an iceberg.

1952

The *United States*, the fastest transatlantic liner of all time, crosses the Atlantic at an average of more than 35 knots to take the "Blue Riband" trophy.

1955

The US submarine *Nautilus*, the first vessel ever to be propelled by nuclear reactor, puts to sea. In 1958 she becomes the first ship ever to reach the North Pole.

1955

Sir Christopher Cockerill patents the design of the hovercraft. A full scale craft makes its first "flight" four years later.

1965

The first regular containership service across the North Atlantic begins.

1969

The world's first barge-carrying vessel, *Acadia Forest*, is built in Japan.

1973

Oil prices are quadrupled, greatly increasing the cost of ship's fuel and hastening the design of slower and more economical ships.

1976

A French shipyard delivers the 550,000-ton capacity crude oil carrier *Battilus*, which was the largest mobile object ever made by man.

1977

Soviet nuclear-powered icebreaker *Arktika* smashes her way to the North Pole.

1978

The very large crude oil carrier *Amoco Cadiz* grounds on the French coast spilling 200,000 tons of oil.

1985

P&O takes delivery of the new cruise ship *Royal Princess*, at $210 million the most expensive merchant ship ever built.

Glossary

Ballast Sea water pumped aboard a ship or submarine to enable it to sink lower in the water, or to submerge it in the case of a submarine.

Diesel engine An engine which burns heavy oil by means of compression and then ignition.

Electromagnetic generation Highly advanced technology which puts a magnetic charge into the sea around a ship to enable a vessel to slip rapidly through it.

Gantry A long-legged crane able to straddle a ship's deck, a stack of containers, or a shipyard building dock.

Guard rings Electronic warning device on a radar display which can give an audible warning of the approach of another ship.

Hydraulics The use of a liquid to transmit force by, for example, driving a piston inside a cylinder.

Ro-ro ship A vessel designed for the carriage of wheeled cargo, or cargo that can be carried aboard by wheeled transport.

Sonar Electronic device using sound waves to detect other ships or undersea obstructions. A vital part of the submariner's equipment.

Straddle carriers Heavy-duty ground-handling equipment used extensively in the container yard to carry and stack containers.

Turbine Propulsion machinery which employs high-pressure steam or gas to rotate blades connected to a driveshaft.

Index

Acknowledgments
The publishers wish to thank the following organizations who have helped in the preparation of this book: British Maritime Technology, British Shipbuilders, Japan Ship Center, Ministry of Defense, Racal Decca (Marine Division) and Wartsila Shipyards, Helsinki.

Photographic Credits
Cover and page 11: Bruce Colman; contents page and page 24: MARS; title page and pages 8-9 and 9: Maritime Institute of the Netherlands; page 8: British Shipbuilders; pages 12, 20, 21 and 23: Ajax News and Features Service; pages 14 and 25: David Higgs; pages 14-15 and 15: Port of Rotterdam; page 16: Evergreen Lines; page 17: Delta Steamship Company; pages 18 and 22: the author; page 19: Racal Decca; pages 20 and 27: Beken of Cowes; pages 26, 28 and 29: Wartsila Shipyards, Helsinki; page 27: Wijsmuller Bureau.